#56
Granada Hills Branch
10640 Petit Avenue
Granada Hills, CA 91344

FEB 0 3 2005

S0-AVW-940

MAR 11 2005

 THE AMERICAN CIVIL WAR

FAMOUS UNION GENERALS AND LEADERS OF THE NORTH

A MyReportLinks.com Book

Pat McCarthy

 MyReportLinks.com Books

an imprint of

 Enslow Publishers, Inc.

Box 398, 40 Industrial Road
Berkeley Heights, NJ 07922
USA

920.073
M1235

MyReportLinks.com Books, an imprint of Enslow Publishers, Inc. MyReportLinks®
is a registered trademark of Enslow Publishers, Inc.

Copyright © 2004 by Enslow Publishers, Inc.

All rights reserved.

No part of this book may be reproduced by any means
without the written permission of the publisher.

Library of Congress Cataloging-in-Publication Data

McCarthy, Pat, 1940–
  Famous Union generals and leaders of the North / Pat McCarthy.
    v. cm. — (The American Civil War)
  Includes bibliographical references and index.
    Contents: "Unconditional surrender" Grant—The northern perspective: preserving the Union—The Union's political leaders—The Union's leading generals.
  ISBN 0-7660-5188-9
  1. Generals—United States—Biography—Juvenile literature. 2. United States. Army—Biography—Juvenile literature. 3. Politicians—United States—Biography—Juvenile literature. 4. United States—History—Civil War, 1861–1865—Causes—Juvenile literature. 5. United States—Politics and government—1861–1865—Juvenile literature. [1. Generals. 2. Politicians. 3. United States—History—Civil War, 1861–1865—Causes. 4. United States—Politics and government—1861–1865.] I. Title. II. American Civil War (Berkeley Heights, N.J.)
  E467.M1135 2004
  973.7'41'0922—dc22
                                2003026321

Printed in the United States of America

10 9 8 7 6 5 4 3 2 1

To Our Readers:
Through the purchase of this book, you and your library gain access to the Report Links that specifically back up this book.
The Publisher will provide access to the Report Links that back up this book and will keep these Report Links up to date on **www.myreportlinks.com** for three years from the book's first publication date.
We have done our best to make sure all Internet addresses in this book were active and appropriate when we went to press. However, the author and the Publisher have no control over, and assume no liability for, the material available on those Internet sites or on other Web sites they may link to.
The usage of the MyReportLinks.com Books Web site is subject to the terms and conditions stated on the Usage Policy Statement on **www.myreportlinks.com**.
A password may be required to access the Report Links that back up this book. The password is found on the bottom of page 4 of this book.
Any comments or suggestions can be sent by e-mail to comments@myreportlinks.com or to the address on the back cover.

Photo Credits: © Clipart.com, p. 26; © Hemera Technologies, Inc., 1997–2001, p. 9 (flags); Library of Congress, pp. 1, 3, 10, 13, 18, 27, 29, 33, 34, 36, 38, 40, 42, 44; Mr. Lincoln's White House, p. 24; MyReportLinks.com Books, pp. 4, back cover; The Gilder Lehrman Institute of American History/The Chicago Historical Society, pp. 16, 20, 23, 31; U.S. Department of the Interior, p. 14.

Cover Photos: Flag, © Clipart.com; all other images, Library of Congress.

Cover Description: Photographs of William Tecumseh Sherman, Ulysses S. Grant, and Abraham Lincoln; print of Battle of Antietam.

Contents

Report Links 4

Famous Generals and Leaders
    of the North Facts 9

1 "Unconditional Surrender" Grant 10

2 The Northern Perspective 12

3 The Union's Political Leaders 21

4 The Union's Leading Generals 30

    Chapter Notes 46

    Further Reading 47

    Index 48

			STOP						
Back	Forward	Stop	Review	Home	Explore	Favorites	History

About MyReportLinks.com Books

MyReportLinks.com Books
Great Books, Great Links, Great for Research!

The Report Links listed on the following four pages can save you hours of research time by **instantly** bringing you to the best Web sites relating to your report topic.

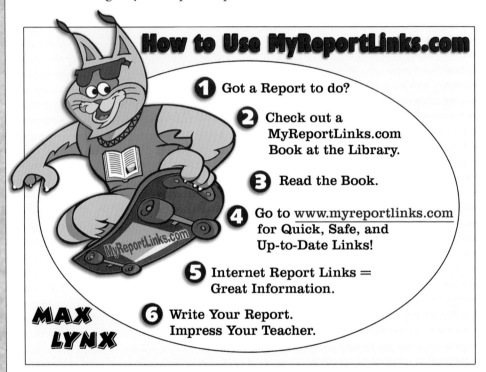

How to Use MyReportLinks.com

1. Got a Report to do?
2. Check out a MyReportLinks.com Book at the Library.
3. Read the Book.
4. Go to www.myreportlinks.com for Quick, Safe, and Up-to-Date Links!
5. Internet Report Links = Great Information.
6. Write Your Report. Impress Your Teacher.

MAX LYNX

The pre-evaluated Web sites are your links to source documents, photographs, illustrations, and maps. They also provide links to dozens—even hundreds—of Web sites about your report subject.

MyReportLinks.com Books and the MyReportLinks.com Web site save you time and make report writing easier than ever!

Please see "To Our Readers" on the copyright page for important information about this book, the MyReportLinks.com Web site, and the Report Links that back up this book. Please enter **WEN4021** if asked for a password.

Report Links

 The Internet sites described below can be accessed at
http://www.myreportlinks.com

▶Northern Leaders
*EDITOR'S CHOICE

On this Web site you can read brief biographies of some of the notable
Northern leaders during the Civil War.

▶American Experience: Ulysses S. Grant
*EDITOR'S CHOICE

This interactive PBS Web site profiles the life of Ulysses S. Grant.
Here you will find a time line, biographies, event descriptions,
Grant's memoirs, and more.

▶Abraham Lincoln (1861–1865)
*EDITOR'S CHOICE

Abraham Lincoln was president of the United States during the Civil
War. His life and presidency are examined in this site.

▶The History Place: A Nation Divided— The U.S. Civil War 1861–1865
*EDITOR'S CHOICE

This Web site provides a time line of the major events of the Civil War.

▶The American Civil War Homepage
*EDITOR'S CHOICE

This site features a list of online Civil War resources. Biographies,
military facts, images, documents, and other kinds of information
are included.

▶A House Divided: America in the Age of Lincoln
*EDITOR'S CHOICE

This online exhibit focuses on American history and culture during the
years of Abraham Lincoln's presidency. Slavery and the Civil War are
covered in depth.

Report Links

The Internet sites described below can be accessed at
http://www.myreportlinks.com

▶**Charles Sumner**

Charles Sumner was one of the most powerful United States senators in the age of
Lincoln and during Reconstruction. Here you will find a biography and quotations.

▶**The Compromise of 1850 and the Fugitive Slave Act**

The Compromise of 1850 briefly smoothed over some of the differences between the
North and South on issues of new territories and slavery, but it also angered
abolitionists. Here you will find a brief description of the compromise.

▶**Crisis at Fort Sumter**

This Tulane University site offers an in-depth look at the crisis at Fort Sumter.
The causes and effects of the conflict can be found here.

▶**Emancipation Proclamation**

The Emancipation Proclamation was issued by Abraham Lincoln in September 1862,
following the Union victory at Antietam, and it became effective January 1, 1863.
This site includes a history of the proclamation and drafts of its text.

▶**Frederick Douglass—1818–1895**

This PBS site contains a brief biography of Frederick Douglass, an important figure in
the fight against slavery.

▶**General George Brinton McClellan**

This Web site provides a biography of General George Brinton McClellan, commander
of the Army of the Potomac during the early years of the war.

▶**George H. Thomas**

General George H. Thomas was one of the Union army's most brilliant leaders.
This Web site includes a chronology of his life as well as links to related articles
and even Civil War music.

▶**George H. Thomas Source Page and Photo Gallery**

General George H. Thomas led the Army of the Cumberland in its successful
southeastern campaign. Here you will find photographs, biographical materials,
and in-depth battle descriptions.

Any comments? Contact us: **comments@myreportlinks.com**

Report Links

The Internet sites described below can be accessed at http://www.myreportlinks.com

▶**John Brown's Holy War**

This PBS site contains the story of the ardent abolitionist John Brown and the Harpers Ferry raid. Interactive maps, videos, biographies, and other resources can be found here.

▶**The Kansas-Nebraska Act and the Rise of the Republican Party, 1854–1856**

This Lincoln Library article contains information about the Kansas-Nebraska Act and its effect on American politics.

▶**Matthew Brady's Portraits**

Matthew Brady was one of the first photographers to capture a war in photographs. Here you will find several of his portraits of Union generals and politicians.

▶**The Meade Archive**

General George Meade was the commander of the Army of the Potomac during the Battle of Gettysburg. Here you will find a biography of Meade, photographs, and a number of other resources.

▶**Missouri Compromise (1820)**

The Missouri Compromise admitted Missouri as a slave state and Maine as a free state. Here you will find the original document, a transcript, and some background information on this legislation.

▶**Mr. Lincoln's White House: Residents and Visitors**

This site offers a profile of the people who played key roles in Abraham Lincoln's White House, including the members of Lincoln's cabinet as well as a number of other important politicians and military figures.

▶**Personal Memoirs of U. S. Grant**

The complete text of the *Personal Memoirs of U.S. Grant* is presented in this site. Grant's story of his life during the Civil War is considered one of the great military narratives of all time.

▶**President Abraham Lincoln's Second Inaugural Address (1865)**

President Lincoln's Second Inaugural Address is one of the most important speeches in the history of the United States. Lincoln's handwritten draft, a transcription, and background on the speech are also included.

Report Links

The Internet sites described below can be accessed at http://www.myreportlinks.com

▶**Salmon P. Chase**

Salmon P. Chase served as both the secretary of the treasury and Chief Justice of the United States during the Lincoln administration. Here you will find his biography.

▶**Slavery in America**

This site takes a comprehensive look at slavery in the United States. Links to sources on the history, geography, and literature of slavery can be found here as well as links to slave narratives.

▶**The Time of the Lincolns**

This wide-ranging PBS site is dedicated to American life during the time of Abraham and Mary Lincoln. Topics such as politics, social issues, and war are covered here.

▶**The Ulysses S. Grant Association**

Here you will find Ulysses S. Grant's photographs, his complete memoirs, and a variety of other resources on the famous Civil War general and American president.

▶**Washington University Libraries: The Dred Scott Case**

Dred Scott was a slave who sued the United States for his freedom. This site features the text of the legal proceedings in Scott's suit as well as a biography of Scott.

▶**William Seward**

William H. Seward was Abraham Lincoln's secretary of state. Here you will learn about his prolific political career.

▶**William Tecumseh Sherman**

An interesting biography of General William Tecumseh Sherman is featured in this Web site.

▶**Winfield Scott**

This Web site provides a brief biography of Winfield Scott, who was general-in-chief of the United States Army when the Civil War began.

Famous Generals and Leaders of the North Facts

Famous Union Generals

Ulysses S. Grant (originally Hiram Ulysses Grant) Born Point Pleasant, Ohio, 1822; died 1882. General given command of all U.S. armies in March 1864; elected eighteenth president of the United States in 1868.

George Brinton McClellan Born Philadelphia 1826; died 1885. General who was both general-in-chief and commanded the Army of the Potomac, 1861–1862.

George Gordon Meade Born Cádiz, Spain, 1815; died 1872. General and commander of the Army of the Potomac, 1863–1865.

William Tecumseh Sherman Born Lancaster, Ohio, 1820; died 1891. General who commanded the military division of the Mississippi (1865) and succeeded Grant as general-in-chief of the army (1869); famous for his march through Georgia.

George Henry Thomas Born Southampton County, Virginia, 1816; died 1870. General who earned the nickname "the Rock of Chickamauga" for valiant defense of his position in Battle of Chickamauga, 1863.

Famous Political Leaders of the North

Abraham Lincoln Born near Hodgenville, Kentucky, 1809; died 1865. Sixteenth president of the United States, elected November 1860; reelected November 1864. Led the nation through the Civil War. Assassinated by John Wilkes Booth, April 14, 1865.

Salmon Portland Chase Born in Cornish, New Hampshire, 1808; died 1873. Politician and jurist, served as U.S. senator, governor of Ohio, U.S. secretary of the treasury in Lincoln administration, and Chief Justice of the United States.

Frederick Douglass (originally Fredrick Augustus Washington Bailey) Born Tuckahoe, Maryland, 1817, a slave; escaped slavery 1838; died 1895. Author, lecturer, abolitionist, publisher, adviser to President Lincoln, U.S. Marshal for District of Columbia, U.S. minister to Haiti.

Charles Sumner Born Boston, Massachusetts, 1811; died 1874. Leader of the Radical Republicans in the U.S. Senate; outspoken foe of slavery.

Chapter 1

"Unconditional Surrender" Grant

As a child, Ulysses S. Grant did not dream of becoming a military hero, although that is what he would become by the end of the Civil War. Grant was a graduate of the United States Military Academy at West Point, like most of the military leaders of the Civil War. He had also served with distinction in the Mexican-American War, so when the Civil War began, he offered to command a regiment.

Grant's offers were ignored, however, until June 1861, when he was put in charge of the Twenty-first Illinois Regiment and led them to their first engagement south, in Missouri. During the next four years, Grant would rise in rank from colonel to general-in-chief of U.S. Armies, and he would later be elected president of the United States

◀ *Ulysses S. Grant at Cold Harbor, Virginia, June 1864.*

on the strength of his heroism during the Civil War. Grant would write in his memoirs, however, that "A military life had no charms for me."[1]

In August 1861, President Abraham Lincoln appointed Grant brigadier general of volunteers, but the early battles he fought were neither well planned nor successful.

In February 1862, while serving under General Henry W. Halleck, Grant convinced him that he should move against the Confederate forces holding Forts Donelson and Henry on the Cumberland and Tennessee Rivers in Tennessee. With seventeen thousand men and the help of gunboats commanded by Commodore Andrew Hull Foote, Grant captured Fort Henry on February 6, and Fort Donelson fell to the North soon after. When General Simon Bolivar Buckner, the Confederate commander at Fort Donelson, asked for Grant's terms of surrender, Grant's answer was, "No terms except an unconditional and immediate surrender can be accepted."[2]

Buckner surrendered fourteen thousand men, and Grant's victories in Tennessee were the first major victories for the North in the Civil War. The Union press seized upon Grant's initials, U. S., and began referring to him as "Unconditional Surrender" Grant.

In 1864, following battles at Shiloh, Vicksburg, and Chattanooga, Grant was put in charge of all Union forces when he was named general-in-chief of the U.S. Armies, a position that had been held by three other generals during the war: Winfield Scott, George McClellan, and Henry Halleck. President Abraham Lincoln, after years of frustration with the men in command of the Union forces, sought in Grant someone who would come up with a strategy to defeat the Confederate army. The president would not be disappointed in his choice.

Chapter 2

The Northern Perspective

The issue of slavery and the question of states' rights divided the United States long before shots rang out over Fort Sumter, in Charleston Harbor, on the morning of April 12, 1861. Differences between North and South had existed since the earliest days of the nation, and those differences grew as the nation grew. What was at stake for the South when the Civil War began was the preservation of a way of life that depended on slave labor. What was at stake for the North, however, was the preservation of the Union—which finally involved the abolition of slavery.

▶ A Peculiar Institution

Southern plantation owners believed that slavery was necessary for their way of life. At the time of the Civil War, cotton was "king"—the main industry in the South. Slaves did most of the work on the largest cotton plantations, and Southerners believed that if they could not use slaves, the cotton industry would be doomed.

Most Northerners opposed slavery, whether on moral, religious, or practical grounds. Since slavery had already been abolished in the Northern states before the Civil War, it was not an important part of the North's economy. Those who opposed slavery were known as abolitionists because they wanted to abolish, or end, the institution. Most believed that it was wrong for one human being to

▲ *These slaves were photographed in Cumberland Landing, Virginia, in the summer of 1862. The question of slavery and its expansion divided the country for years before the Civil War.*

own another, and they banded together, forming societies to try to end slavery.

Other Northerners wanted to limit the expansion of slavery into new territories and new states. Some Northerners, however, backed slavery. The North was the site of the country's textile mills, where cotton was made into cloth. Without slaves, cotton production would decrease, and without cotton, those mills would not be able to make cloth.

Tied to the question of slavery was a basic difference in the way that the leaders of the North and the South perceived the rights of states versus the rights of the federal government. In the years leading up to the Civil War,

several key pieces of legislation addressed that question and the question of slavery's expansion into new territories.

▶ The Missouri Compromise

When the Missouri Territory, which was home to many slaves, applied to become a state in 1819, a bitter battle erupted in Congress over the expansion of slavery. At the time, there were eleven free states and eleven slave states in the Union. If Missouri were admitted as a slave state, that balance would be upset. Congressman James Tallmadge of New York, concerned that the South would hold a congressional advantage, proposed admitting Missouri as a slave state but limiting the importation of slaves there and eventually freeing all slaves born in Missouri.

To resolve the issue, a compromise was reached in 1820 that eventually admitted Missouri as a slave state

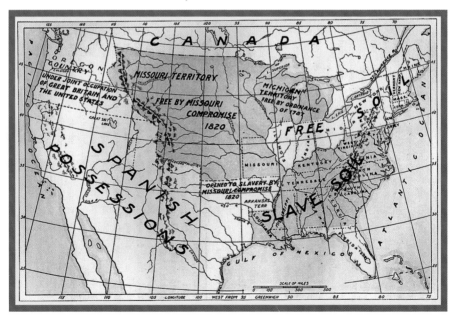

▲ This map shows the division of free states, slave states, and free territories that existed in the United States in 1820, the year of the Missouri Compromise.

and Maine, which had been part of Massachusetts, as a free state. The Senate agreed to combine the applications of the two states in a single bill and add an amendment that prohibited slavery in the rest of the Louisiana Territory above 36 degrees 30 minutes north latitude. As a measure that strengthened the power of the federal government, the Missouri Compromise was viewed favorably by Northerners. Southerners, meanwhile, were unhappy with any limits to slavery, which they considered a violation of the sovereignty of states.

The United States continued to expand its territory. Between 1820 and 1850, six states entered the Union. Three of them, Arkansas, Florida, and Texas, entered as slave states. The other three, Michigan, Iowa, and Wisconsin, were free states. The balance between free and slave states was soon to be in jeopardy again, and the division between the North and South over the question of slavery would once again result in congressional debate and compromise.

The Compromise of 1850

In 1850, California wanted to join the Union as a free state. The United States had just fought a war with Mexico and, as a result, had acquired a large amount of land. A debate again raged over whether slavery should be allowed in these new territories.

To resolve the issue, the congressional leaders of the North and South reached another compromise, the Compromise of 1850. California was admitted to the Union as a free state, while the territories of New Mexico, Nevada, Arizona, and Utah were organized as places where the question of slavery would be decided by the territories' settlers once they were ready for statehood.

To appease Southerners, a tough Fugitive Slave Law was attached, requiring citizens to turn in runaway slaves and making it a federal crime to help slaves escape. The law made Northerners furious, however, and Northern state governments passed their own personal-liberty laws that violated the provisions of the Compromise of 1850. The uneasy truce between North and South would not last for long, however.

The Kansas-Nebraska Act

In 1854, the Kansas-Nebraska Act created two more territories in the land west of the Mississippi. The terms of the

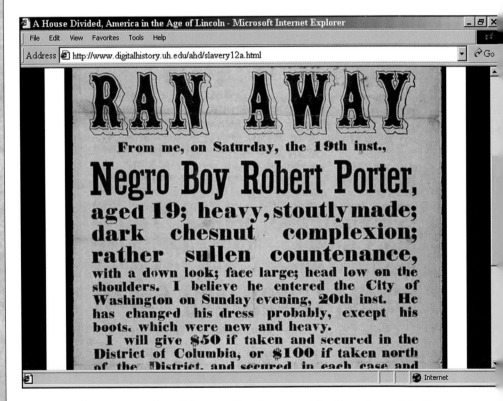

Posters such as this one offered a reward for the return of fugitive slaves. Under the Fugitive Slave Law that was passed in 1850, any white man, North or South, could seize a slave who had escaped.

Missouri Compromise had forbidden slavery in these lands, but the terms of the Kansas-Nebraska Act redrew the boundaries for slavery that had existed since 1820. The act provided for popular sovereignty, which meant that the white settlers of the territories of Kansas and Nebraska could decide for themselves whether to permit slavery once the territories became states. Southerners hailed the act as a victory for states' rights and slavery. Northerners considered it enough of a threat to have formed a political party, the Republican party, in reaction to it. Disagreements between proslavery and antislavery groups in Kansas led to violence and bloodshed in the territory, which came to be called "Bleeding Kansas."

Dred Scott Decision

The question of slavery and its expansion continued to divide the country in the 1850s as a Supreme Court decision dealt the Missouri Compromise a final blow. In 1857, the Supreme Court ruled in the Dred Scott decision that Scott, a slave who sued for his freedom on the basis that he had lived for a time in a free territory, was not a citizen. The Court further ruled the Missouri Compromise unconstitutional, stating that the federal government had no right to ban slavery in a territory. Abolitionists and other Northerners were angered by the decision, while Southerners hailed it.

John Brown's Attack on Harpers Ferry

On October 16, 1859, John Brown, a radical abolitionist born in Connecticut, led a band of blacks and whites in a raid on the federal arsenal at Harpers Ferry, Virginia. The next day, United States Marines stormed the arsenal and captured or killed most of Brown's men. Brown himself

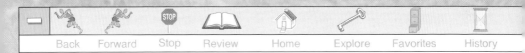

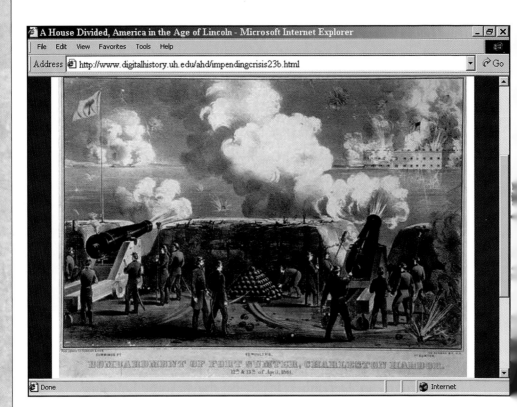

A House Divided, America in the Age of Lincoln - Microsoft Internet Explorer

File   Edit   View   Favorites   Tools   Help

Address http://www.digitalhistory.uh.edu/ahd/impendingcrisis23b.html   Go

Done   Internet

▲ *On April 12, 1861, Confederate troops led by General P.G.T. Beauregard opened fire on Fort Sumter, in Charleston Harbor. Major Robert Anderson of the United States Army was forced to surrender, and the Civil War was under way.*

President Lincoln felt he had no choice but to call for troops. He considered secession unconstitutional and acts of violence to support secession as revolutionary acts. Lincoln declared that he would enforce the laws and occupy federal property in the states that had seceded. The Civil War had begun.

Chapter 3 ►

The Union's Political Leaders

Abraham Lincoln was the president of the United States and commander-in-chief of its armed forces during the years of the Civil War, 1861 to 1865. He was the man most responsible for reuniting the country and preserving the Union. The political leaders of the Union, including Lincoln, did not think that the war would last long since the North had two great advantages—it had twice as many people and the bulk of the nation's industry. But Lincoln and his military advisers were proven wrong, as the war dragged out for four long years—and brought with it a loss of life that was staggering. Nearly 2 percent of the American population at the time perished in the American Civil War. Lincoln's leadership in a time of great national crisis has led him to be regarded by many historians as one of our greatest presidents. He worked to strengthen the new Republican party while rallying Northern Democrats to support the Union cause. His leadership was even more remarkable when one considers that some of his own generals failed to take advantage of situations that could have ended the war sooner.

The bloodiest single day of the war came on September 17, 1862, during the Battle of Antietam, in Maryland, the Confederate army's first advance into Northern territory. The battle was considered a Union victory because Union general George B. McClellan checked the advance of Robert E. Lee's army and forced it to retreat south. But it is also widely believed that if

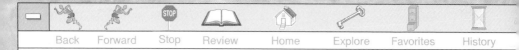
McClellan had pursued Lee's army, the war might have ended that day. Lincoln, frustrated with McClellan's hesitation and cautiousness on the battlefield, replaced him with Ambrose Burnside, who was more decisive but no more effective a leader. It was not until Lincoln named Ulysses S. Grant as general-in-chief of the United States Armies in 1864 that he finally had a commanding general with a plan that worked to end the war.

The costly victory at Antietam did give Lincoln the victory he needed to issue the Emancipation Proclamation, which became effective on January 1, 1863. This document proclaimed the slaves within the Confederacy free, but it did not apply to slaves in the border states, and in reality it freed no one, since the Confederacy was not bound by the laws of the United States at the time. What it did do, and what Lincoln had hoped to accomplish, was to add a new urgency to the fight for the Union army. It also added new recruits, since African Americans were allowed to enlist beginning in 1863.

Lincoln was reelected president in 1864 while the war raged on. In his second inaugural address, he urged Southerners to stop fighting and become part of the Union again. He promised to work with them to try to "bind up the nation's wounds."[1] But he would never have the chance: His death at the hands of John Wilkes Booth only five days after Lee's surrender to Grant at Appomattox Court House left the nation without its leader.

▶ Salmon P. Chase

Salmon Portland Chase was a lawyer and antislavery leader from Ohio who served as secretary of the treasury and then Chief Justice of the United States Supreme Court during Lincoln's administration.

Chase was born in New Hampshire but moved to Ohio when he was nine. After his father died, he was cared for by his uncle, who was the Episcopal bishop of Ohio. Chase began college in Cincinnati but soon transferred to Dartmouth, where he graduated with honors.

Chase moved to Washington, D.C., where he ran a school for boys while studying law with United States Attorney General William Wirt. After Chase was admitted to the bar, he went back to Ohio to practice law and became involved in the abolitionist movement there. He defended so many slaves who had escaped that he became

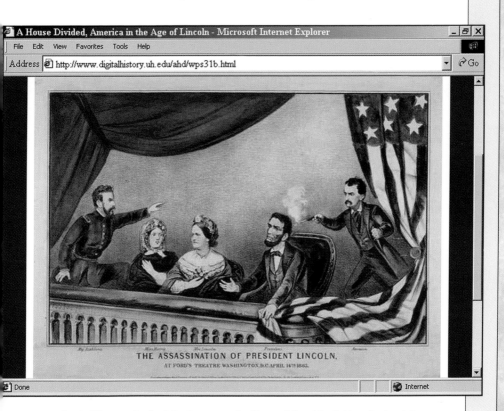

A House Divided, America in the Age of Lincoln - Microsoft Internet Explorer

File   Edit   View   Favorites   Tools   Help

Address http://www.digitalhistory.uh.edu/ahd/wps31b.html

THE ASSASSINATION OF PRESIDENT LINCOLN,
AT FORD'S THEATRE WASHINGTON, D.C. APRIL 14TH 1865.

Done   Internet

▲ A lithograph depicts the assassination of President Lincoln by John Wilkes Booth at Ford's Theatre on the evening of April 14, 1865. Pictured with Lincoln, from left to right, are Major H. R. Rathbone, Miss Clara Harris, and Mary Todd Lincoln, the First Lady.

known as the "attorney general" for fugitive slaves. An extremely religious man, he considered slavery to be morally wrong and he believed African Americans should be allowed to vote. He once stated, "True democracy makes no inquiry about the color of the skin, or the places of nativity [birth], or any other similar circumstances of condition. Whenever it sees a man, it recognizes a being endowed by his Creator with original inalienable rights . . . I regard, therefore, the exclusion of colored people from the election franchise as incompatible with true democratic principles."[2]

Chase served in the United States Senate from 1849 to 1855, where he strongly opposed both the Compromise

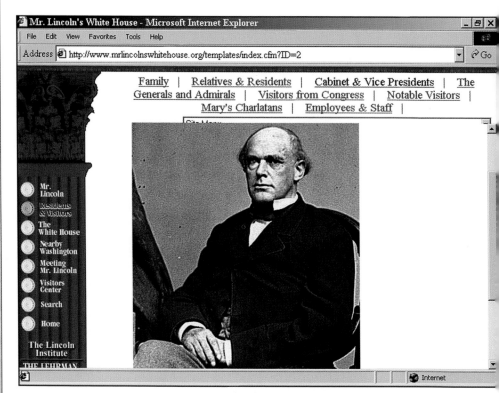

Salmon P. Chase, Lincoln's secretary of the treasury, had the unenviable job of trying to come up with the money needed to fight the war and keep the federal government operating at the same time.

of 1850 and the Kansas-Nebraska Act. Chase was then twice elected governor of Ohio, in 1856 and 1858. In both 1856 and 1860, he tried to secure the Republican nomination for president. When Lincoln was elected president, he appointed Chase his secretary of the treasury.

In that position, Chase was responsible for coming up with the funds needed to operate the government while financing the war, which involved collecting new taxes and placing large loans with investors who were reluctant to cover them. To improve the country's currency, Chase established the national banking system in 1863, which is often considered his greatest achievement.

Chase's ambitions and his more radical views on abolition strained his relationship with Abraham Lincoln, however, and in 1864, the president finally accepted Chase's resignation. When Chief Justice Roger Taney died, Lincoln appointed Salmon P. Chase to replace Taney as Chief Justice of the United States.

▶ Charles Sumner

Charles Sumner of Massachusetts was, like Chase, a radical abolitionist. He graduated from Harvard with a law degree and served in the United States Senate for more than twenty years. Sumner firmly opposed the Fugitive Slave Law and the Kansas-Nebraska Act.

Sumner was known for his strong antislavery speeches in the Senate, which angered the proslavery forces. His most famous speech, "The Crime Against Kansas," delivered over two days, May 19 and 20, 1856, almost cost him his life. In it he attacked Senator Andrew Pickens Butler of South Carolina, who was not present to defend himself. Two days later, Butler's nephew, Preston S. Brooks, assaulted Sumner in the Senate chamber by beating him

⚠ Charles Sumner, an outspoken critic of Southern policies, nearly paid with his life for his verbal attacks on Southern politicians.

with a cane. Sumner's injuries were so severe that it took him more than three years to recover from the attack. When he did, Massachusetts reelected him to the Senate in 1858. Sumner was also a leading figure in helping to organize the new Republican party.

In 1861, Sumner was made chairman of the Senate Committee on Foreign Relations, where he was involved in trying to prevent European intervention in the war on the side of the Confederacy.[3] He became one of the most vocal proponents of the Emancipation Proclamation, although he criticized President Lincoln for delaying it. During Reconstruction, Sumner was the leader in the

Senate of the Radical Republicans. They were a group of congressional leaders who wanted to see the South punished for having seceded.

William Henry Seward

William Henry Seward, born in Florida, New York, in 1801, was a prominent New York politician, serving as governor of that state before being elected to the United States Senate. Firmly opposed to slavery, he voiced his opposition to the Compromise of 1850 and like Lincoln, warned that the country would remain in conflict over the question of slavery. In an 1858 speech in Rochester, New York, he uttered words that became a catchphrase for the abolitionist movement when he commented that there was a "higher law than the Constitution."[4] In 1861, Lincoln named Seward his secretary of state, and Seward expected to exert a great deal of influence in Lincoln's administration. He was disappointed, however, when Lincoln made his own decisions, often not consulting his cabinet or not taking their advice. Seward and Salmon Chase, the secretary of the treasury, were rivals and often at odds with one another.

William Henry Seward proved to be an able secretary of state in the Lincoln administration.

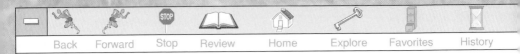
Seward proved to be an able secretary of state once the Civil War began, however. His handling of the *Trent* affair helped keep the United States from becoming involved in two wars at the same time. In that incident, two Confederate commissioners aboard a British steamer, the *Trent*, were traveling to Europe when they were detained and imprisoned by the captain of a Union ship who had not been ordered to do so. Following the protests of British diplomats, Seward released the commissioners and averted a possible war with Great Britain.

It was Seward who convinced Abraham Lincoln not to announce the Emancipation Proclamation until the Union army had gained a major military victory. That victory came in September 1862 at Antietam.

John Wilkes Booth's plot to assassinate President Abraham Lincoln included an attack on Secretary of State Seward, who was stabbed in his bed the same night that Booth shot Lincoln. Unlike the president, however, Seward recovered and continued his position in Andrew Johnson's administration, where in 1867 he arranged for the purchase of Alaska.

▶ Frederick Douglass

Although not a politician, Frederick Douglass, formerly a slave, was a leading abolitionist, editor, and orator in the years before the Civil War, and he served as an adviser to Abraham Lincoln during the war. He was originally critical of the president and pressed for the emancipation of all slaves in the Confederacy and the border states. He also fought for the rights of African Americans to enlist in the Union army to fight for that freedom. Once Congress authorized that enlistment in 1863, Douglass's sons Lewis and Charles were among the first to join, and they

Frederick Douglass, who fought for the civil rights of African Americans, was an eloquent voice for the abolition of slavery.

were followed by their brother, Frederick Jr.

But although they were allowed to enlist, black soldiers were not given equal treatment with white soldiers, and Douglass first met with Lincoln in the summer of 1863 to express his concerns over that treatment. In August 1864, Douglass had a second meeting with Lincoln, who was concerned about how the war was going and feared he might have to sign a truce with the Confederacy that left slavery in place. The president asked Douglass to come up with a plan to lead slaves out of the South in the event that a Union victory never came.

When Douglass tried to attend President Lincoln's reception following Lincoln's second inauguration, government officials refused to allow him or any other African-Amererican man into the White House. When Lincoln found out what had happened, he had Douglass ushered into the ceremony and greeted him in a booming voice with the words "Here comes my friend Douglass."[5]

When Lincoln was assassinated, Douglass mourned the man he had come to consider a friend, but he could not mourn for long because he continued to press for the civil rights of African Americans.

Chapter 4

The Union's Leading Generals

At the start of the Civil War, General Winfield Scott was general-in-chief of the United States Army. Known as "Old Fuss and Feathers" because he was so picky about military regulations and liked to dress up in military finery, Scott had been an excellent general in his time. He distinguished himself in the War of 1812 and the Mexican-American War. But in 1861, Scott was seventy-five years old—too old for active duty. Scott had hoped that Robert E. Lee would succeed him in command, but Lee, a Virginian, chose instead to serve with the Confederacy when Virginia seceded. When Scott retired in November 1861, President Lincoln replaced him with General George B. McClellan. Four men would serve as general-in-chief of the United States Army during the Civil War, but the most important was Ulysses S. Grant. Three other leading generals of the Union army, William Tecumseh Sherman, George Henry Thomas, and George Gordon Meade, would serve under Grant.

▶ General Ulysses S. Grant

Although he commanded the Union army for only the last thirteen months of the Civil War, Ulysses S. Grant was the most influential general for the North. Born in Ohio in 1822, Grant graduated from West Point in 1843 and served honorably in the Mexican-American War. But by 1854, he was forced to resign from the army because of a drinking problem. He tried his hand at farming and in business, but failed at both. When the Civil War began, he was employed in his family's leather store in Galena, Illinois. His offer to command a regiment was rejected, but Grant was commissioned a colonel of the Twenty-first Illinois Regiment. By August 1861, he was made a brigadier general of volunteers. The North's first major victory in the war came under Grant's command at Forts Henry and Donelson in Tennessee in February 1862, and Grant was promoted to major general of volunteers following those battles. In April, his troops suffered heavy casualties at the Battle of Shiloh, which took place outside Pittsburg Landing, Tennessee. Reinforcements by

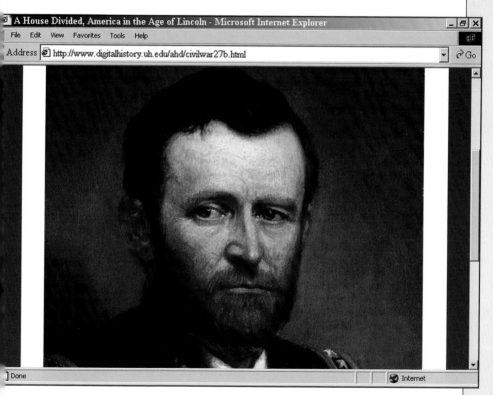

A House Divided, America in the Age of Lincoln - Microsoft Internet Explorer

File   Edit   View   Favorites   Tools   Help

Address http://www.digitalhistory.uh.edu/ahd/civilwar27b.html   Go

Done   Internet

▲ *There was nothing in Ulysses S. Grant's life before the Civil War that would have led anyone to foresee the success he would have in waging war against the Confederacy.*

Generals Don Carlos Buell and Lew Wallace, however, allowed the Union army to loosen the hold the Confederate army had on Tennessee.

Grant's greatest strategic success came in the Vicksburg campaign, which was waged from November 1862 to July 1863. Vicksburg, Mississippi, was a key port on the Mississippi River, and the Union army fought to control the river to split the Confederacy in half and restore commerce to cities in the Northwest. When by May 1863, Grant realized that the heavily fortified city could not be taken by storming it, he devised a plan to starve it, cutting off its supply lines and its communications with the outside world. Confederate general John C. Pemberton surrendered to Ulysses S. Grant on July 4, 1863, a day after the Union victory at the Battle of Gettysburg. Grant was then made commander of the military division of the Mississippi.

Grant next claimed victories in November at Lookout Mountain and Missionary Ridge in Tennessee. Finally finding in Grant the commander he had sought throughout the war, Lincoln named him commander of all Union armies in March 1864, and Grant was promoted to lieutenant general, a military rank that Congress brought back into being especially for him. Grant chose to make his headquarters with the Army of the Potomac, where he directed General George G. Meade.

Grant waged a war of attrition against Robert E. Lee's Army of Northern Virginia, causing heavy casualties in the Confederate ranks, which were already severely depleted and undersupplied. The Union army suffered heavy casualties in the battles of the Wilderness, Spotsylvania, and Cold Harbor in Virginia, but the Confederate army suffered irreplaceable losses, since the Union army was able to supply reinforcements and the Confederate army was not. Following those battles, Robert E. Lee was never able to take the offensive again.

Grant moved south to Petersburg, where his armies lay siege from June 1864 to April 1865. Petersburg guarded the southern approaches to Richmond, and Grant's siege forced Robert E. Lee to defend Petersburg in order to protect the Confederate capital. Both Petersburg and Richmond fell to Union forces on April 3. The Confederate army retreated, and Grant pushed on.

General Ulysses S. Grant sent General Robert E. Lee a letter that respectfully requested his surrender, which Lee initially refused. But following a brief battle, Lee agreed to meet Grant on April 9, 1865, to surrender at Appomattox Court House. Knowing how much the Southern armies had suffered and lost, Grant's terms were generous: He would allow Confederate officers to keep their pistols and allow soldiers who owned horses to take them with them. Grant required his men to treat the men of the Confederate army at Appomattox with dignity.

Grant was hailed as the man who had won the war for the Union, and that

General Ulysses S. Grant in 1865, the final year of the Civil War.

popularity led to his being elected president of the United States in November 1868. Grant served two terms as president as the nation struggled through Reconstruction. An able general, he was less able as a politician, and scandals rocked his administration, although he was not personally responsible for them. After leaving office, he became involved in a number of unsuccessful business ventures, losing most of his money. Ulysses S. Grant decided to write his memoirs to help provide for his family. While writing them, he was diagnosed with throat cancer. He died just a few days after finishing them. They are considered one of the greatest military narratives ever published.

General William Tecumseh Sherman

Like Ulysses S. Grant, William Tecumseh Sherman was a native of Ohio. And like Grant, Sherman was a realist about war, which may be why he excelled at it. Sherman was a West Point graduate and served in California during the Mexican-American War. He resigned his commission in 1853 and was involved in several unsuccessful business ventures. In 1859, Sherman became the superintendent of the Louisiana State Seminary and Military Academy, but he resigned that position in January 1861 when talk of secession became more serious.

To many Georgians, William Tecumseh Sherman remains "the most hated man in Georgia" long after his march through that state during the Civil War.

In May 1861, Sherman wrote to the secretary of war and offered his services to the Union army. He was made a colonel in the Thirteenth Regular Infantry and assumed the command of a brigade that came under heavy Confederate fire during the First Battle of Bull Run in July. In August, he was promoted to brigadier general and served in Missouri and Kentucky for the remainder of 1861 and into 1862. During this time, Sherman was known to argue with the press and was even labeled by some as insane. It was after this ordeal that Sherman began his long and successful association with General Ulysses S. Grant.

In April 1862, Sherman led his men valiantly as a division commander during the bloody Battle of Shiloh and was promoted to major general the following month. Grant made sure that Sherman was part of the Vicksburg campaign in 1863, where in the first advance Sherman suffered defeat but later served ably as the commander of the Fifteenth Corps. Following Vicksburg, Sherman was made a brigadier general in the regular army.

Sherman became commander of the Army of the Tennessee, succeeding Grant in October 1863 after Grant assumed supreme command in the West. Sherman fought in the Chattanooga campaign in November, went to the rescue of General Ambrose Burnside in Knoxville in December, and in February 1864, dealt the Confederacy a blow when he destroyed Confederate communications and supplies at Meridian, Mississippi. When Grant was made commander of all Union forces in March, Sherman again succeeded him and became supreme commander in the West.

Sherman then embarked upon the campaign that earned him the greatest fame and consideration as one of

▲ *The strategy of total war that brought devastation to the South was devised by Ulysses S. Grant but put into practice by William Tecumseh Sherman, above.*

the Union army's greatest strategists and most influential generals. In the Atlanta campaign, Sherman was ordered by Grant to "create havoc and destruction of all resources that would be beneficial to the enemy."[1] Directed by Grant and put into practice by Sherman, this modern strategy of total war would affect civilians as well as soldiers, as the Confederacy was cut in half and its citizens and troops were cut off from supplies.

In May 1864, Sherman began his march toward Atlanta, Georgia, with nearly 100,000 men. Before reaching that city, he engaged in battles with Joseph

E. Johnston's troops, who were able to skillfully retreat when needed. But Johnston was replaced by John Bell Hood, and Sherman and his men soundly defeated him and captured Atlanta on the second of September. Sherman burned most of the city, and the next day began his "march to the sea" toward Savannah, as he and his men left a ruined and devastated land in their wake. Sherman then advanced northward through South Carolina, leaving that state—the first state to have seceded—even more devastated than Georgia.

William Tecumseh Sherman would again succeed Ulysses S. Grant. In 1869, with Grant president, Sherman was made commander of the United States Army. He retired in 1884, and resisted all efforts to be drawn into politics. In addition to his military achievements, Sherman is remembered as a man of few, but choice, words, such as his often-repeated phrase "War is hell," which he delivered in an 1879 speech to cadets at the Michigan Military Academy.

General George Henry Thomas

George Henry Thomas was born in Southampton County, Virginia, on July 31, 1816. When he was fifteen years old, he and his family fled their farm during the Southampton Insurrection, a slave revolt led by Nat Turner. Thomas attended the United States Military Academy at West Point, where he graduated twelfth in his class. His roommate during his plebe, or first, year was William Tecumseh Sherman. A veteran of the Seminole and Mexican-American Wars, Thomas became an instructor in cavalry and artillery at the academy at West Point in 1851, where his students included Philip Sheridan and J.E.B. Stuart, who would become generals in the Union

General George Thomas was one of the few members of the military from Virginia who chose to remain loyal to the Union. Admiral David Farragut was another.

and Confederate armies, respectively. Thomas was posted in California and Texas and in 1860 he was wounded by an arrow during a skirmish with Comanche Indians on the Texas frontier. When the Civil War began, Thomas chose to remain with the Union, unlike fellow Virginian Robert E. Lee. It was a decision that cost Thomas professionally and personally: His sisters, who were loyal to the Confederacy, disowned him.

Promoted to colonel in May 1861, he commanded the Second U.S. Cavalry in Pennsylvania, where he led them in several battles in the Shenandoah Valley. In August he was promoted to brigadier general of volunteers for the Department of the Cumberland, where he commanded and trained six thousand volunteers from Kentucky and Tennessee. It was the beginning of the Army of the Cumberland, which would number 60,000 at its height. In January 1862, Thomas earned an important victory at Mill Springs, Kentucky, that denied the Confederates access to the Cumberland Gap. He was promoted to major general of U.S. volunteers and early in 1863 was given command of the Fourteenth Corps,

Army of the Cumberland, after contributing to the Union victory at Stones River, Tennessee.

During the campaign to take Chattanooga, Tennessee, a key city on the rail line that supplied Confederates with materials, Thomas was involved in a battle in Georgia that would have resulted in a rout if not for his efforts. Although it was a Union defeat, the Battle of Chickamauga earned Thomas the nickname "the Rock of Chickamauga" when on September 20, 1863, Thomas and his men stubbornly held Snodgrass Hill during the second day of the battle while they were repeatedly under attack. The Chattanooga campaign continued with Thomas as the commander of the Army of the Cumberland. In November, his army broke through General Bragg's Confederate line at Missionary Ridge and helped Ulysses S. Grant to earn a victory at the Battle of Chattanooga.

After Atlanta fell to Sherman's army, Thomas was sent to try to stop General John Bell Hood's troops, which were attacking General Sherman's supply lines. At the Battle of Nashville in December 1864, Thomas used cavalry as a key part of his offensive strategy. His victory and pursuit of Hood's army afterward signaled the final destruction of the Confederates' main western army. Thomas was promoted to major general and in March 1865 received the Thanks of Congress, a high honor, for the victory at Nashville.

Thomas remained in command in Tennessee until 1867, when he was assigned to command on the Pacific Coast. During a ceremony in which he was presented with a gold medal by the governor of Tennessee to mark the second anniversary of the Battle of Nashville, Thomas

▲ *This print captures General George Thomas's charge near Orchard Knob during the Battle of Chattanooga, November 24, 1863.*

offered a simple but eloquent explanation why he had remained with the Union at the war's outset:

Some thirty years ago I received my diploma at the Military Academy, and soon after a commission in the Army. On receiving that commission I took an oath to sustain the Constitution of the United States, and the Government, and to obey all officers of the Government placed over me. I have faithfully endeavored to keep that oath. I did not regard it so much as an oath, but as a solemn pledge on my part to return the Government some little service for the great benefit I had received in obtaining my education at the Academy.[2]

▶ General George B. McClellan

George Brinton McClellan was a West Point graduate who had served in the Mexican-American War with distinction and had worked on several engineering projects, including a survey for a rail route in the Cascade Range in the American West before the Civil War. A brilliant engineer, he would prove to be less brilliant as a field commander, although he retained the loyalty of the men who served under him. He was also responsible in large part for organizing the Army of the Potomac and seeing that it was supplied with the materials it would need to fight.

McClellan was made commander of the Department of the Ohio in May 1861 and commissioned a major general in the regular army. After the Union defeat at the First Battle of Bull Run in July 1861, McClellan was given command of the Army of the Potomac. An ambitious man, he worked to secure the position of general-in-chief, which was held by Winfield Scott. He was given that position in November.

McClellan was pressed to begin an offensive campaign, but he insisted that his troops needed more time to be trained and supplied. He excelled in organizing the Army of the Potomac, but President Lincoln became frustrated with his lack of initiative on the battlefield and considered him too cautious. McClellan also repeatedly overestimated the strength of the Confederate armies he faced and failed to pursue them, allowing the Confederates to bring in reinforcements. In March 1862, McClellan was relieved of his supreme command but retained command of the Army of the Potomac.

By the time McClellan moved the army out of Washington to advance on the Confederates at Manassas,

General George Brinton McClellan excelled at organizing the fledgling Army of the Potomac, which consisted of raw recruits without battle experience when he took over. He was less able a field commander, however.

Virginia, General Joseph Johnston's army had withdrawn. When the army was in its winter headquarters, McClellan came up with a plan. In April 1862, he took his army to the York-James Peninsula to seize Richmond, the Confederate capital, in what was called the Peninsular campaign. Lincoln did not like the plan, since it left Washington, D.C., vulnerable to attack. McClellan's forces reached Yorktown, Virginia, on April 5, but McClellan was convinced that Confederate general John Magruder had many more than his eleven thousand men, and McClellan ignored Lincoln's order to press forward. While McClellan waited, General Joseph Johnston was able to move his entire army onto the peninsula, blocking the Union troops from advancing. Johnston said, "No one but McClellan could have hesitated to attack."[3]

When Union and Confederate forces clashed at the Battle of Seven Pines, Johnston was wounded, and Confederate president Jefferson Davis replaced him with Robert E. Lee. McClellan misjudged Lee completely, saying, "I prefer Lee to Johnston . . . he [Lee] is likely to be timid and irresolute in action."[4]

During a series of bloody battles outside Richmond, Union troops were able to fight off repeated Confederate attacks, but McClellan failed to take advantage, and his army retreated. The Confederate army under Robert E. Lee had suffered heavy casualties, but by taking the offensive, Lee had saved Richmond. McClellan called for more troops, blaming the federal War Department and President Lincoln for his failures.

Following General John Pope's Union defeat at the Second Battle of Bull Run in July 1862, McClellan again reorganized his army and had another chance to defeat Lee during the Battle of Antietam in Maryland in September. That battle resulted in the bloodiest single day of fighting in the war, and Lee's crippled army was backed up against the Potomac River, but McClellan failed to pursue Lee as he retreated south. Lincoln had sent McClellan a telegram, telling him to "Destroy the rebel army if possible," but McClellan refused.[5]

Although Antietam was a strategic victory for the North, Lincoln was furious with McClellan and relieved him of his command of the Army of the Potomac on November 9, 1862. McClellan returned home to Trenton, New Jersey, to await further orders, but none ever came. With his army career finished, McClellan decided to enter politics and became the Democratic nominee for president, running against the Republican nominee and incumbent president, Abraham Lincoln. Lincoln was reelected, and McClellan resigned from the army on the day of the election. He traveled throughout Europe with his family before working as an engineer in New York City. He was elected governor of New Jersey in 1878 and served one term.

General George Gordon Meade

George Gordon Meade, another West Point graduate, was born in Spain of American parents. He resigned from the army in 1836 to pursue a career as a civil engineer, but he reentered the army in 1842 and except for his service during the Mexican-American War, he worked as a military engineer. When the Civil War began, he was assigned command of one of three Pennsylvania brigades and was commissioned a brigadier general of volunteers. He served near Washington, D.C., and in northern Virginia before joining McClellan's Army of the Potomac in the Peninsular campaign. During the Seven Days Battles, Meade was severely wounded twice. Not completely

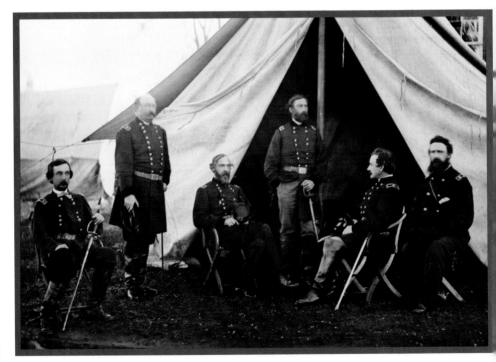

▲ *General George G. Meade, seated third from left, is flanked by fellow generals in the Army of the Potomac. The photograph was taken in Virginia in 1863.*

recovered, he led his brigade at the Second Battle of Bull Run and commanded a division at Fredericksburg. A few days after that battle, he was given command of the Fifth Corps, which he led at the Battle of Chancellorsville. After General Joseph Hooker failed miserably there, Meade was given command of the Army of the Potomac on June 28, 1863. He assumed that command only days before the most pivotal battle of the war was to take place—the Battle of Gettysburg.

During that battle, General Meade cleverly shifted his forces from one site to another, wherever they were most needed. The Union victory at Gettsyburg on July 3, 1863, marked the decline of the Confederate army and changed the course of the war. But Lee's army was allowed to retreat south across the Potomac River after initially being trapped against the river, which was swollen from heavy rain. Meade was criticized for not adequately pursuing Lee and offered to resign, but his resignation was not accepted, and he was made a brigadier general in the regular army.

Although he continued to command the Army of the Potomac for the remainder of the war, his actions were really directed by Ulysses S. Grant once Grant was made general-in-chief in March 1864, since Grant chose to make his headquarters with the Army of the Potomac. On Grant's recommendation, Meade was made a major general of the Union army in August 1864. Meade then commanded several military departments in the East and South following the war. He was in charge of the Military Division of the Atlantic, which was based in Philadelphia, at the time of his death on November 6, 1872.

Chapter Notes

Chapter 1. "Unconditional Surrender" Grant

1. Ulysses S. Grant, *Personal Memoirs of U.S. Grant* (New York: C.L.Webster and Company, 1885), p. 13.

2. Geoffrey Perret, *Ulysses S. Grant: Soldier and President* (New York: Random House, 1997), p. 173.

Chapter 2. The Northern Perspective

1. David Herbert Donald, *Lincoln* (New York: Simon and Schuster, 1995), p. 206.

2. Allen C. Guelzo, *Abraham Lincoln: Redeemer President* (Grand Rapids, Mich.: William B. Eerdmans Publishing Company, 1999), p. 253.

3. Ibid.

Chapter 3. The Union's Political Leaders

1. Allen C. Guelzo, *Abraham Lincoln: Redeemer President* (Grand Rapids, Mich.: William B. Eerdmans Publishing Company, 1999), p. 420.

2. "Salmon Portland Chase: Attorney General of Fugitive Slaves," n.d., <http://pw1.netcom.com/~rilydia/chase/spchase1.html> (March 8, 2004).

3. "Charles Sumner, an Abolitionist in Politics," *The African American Registry*, n.d., <http://www.aaregistry.com/african_american_history/2199/Charles_Sumner_an_abolitionist_in_politics> (March 5, 2004).

4. "William H. Seward," n.d., <http://www.tulane.edu/~latner/Seward.html> (March 23, 2004).

5. Allen Thorndike Rice, ed., *Reminiscences of Abraham Lincoln by Distinguished Men of His Time* (New York: The North American Review, 1885), pp. 191–93.

Chapter 4. The Union's Leading Generals

1. Wayne C. Bengston, "William Tecumseh Sherman: A North Georgia Notable," *About North Georgia*, n.d., <http://ngeorgia.com/people/shermanwt.html> (March 8, 2004).

2. Wilbur Thomas, *General George H. Thomas: The Indomitable Warrior* (New York: Exposition Press, 1964), p. 605.

3. "Major General George McClellan," *The American Civil War*, n.d., <http://www.swcivilwar.com/mcclellan.html> (March 8, 2004).

4. Ibid., p. 4.

5. "Reports of Major General George B. McClellan," *Home of the American Civil War*, n.d., <http://www.civilwarhome.com/mcclellanantietam3or.htm> (March 8, 2004).

Further Reading

Adelson, Bruce. *George Meade: Union General.* Broomall, Pa.: Chelsea House Publishers, 2001.

Cothran, Helen. *Abraham Lincoln.* Farmington Hills, Mich.: Gale Group, 2002.

Donald, David Herbert. *Charles Sumner.* New York: Da Capo Press, 1996.

Green, Carl R., and William R. Sanford. *Union Generals of the Civil War.* Springfield, N.J.: Enslow Publishers, 1998.

Head, Tom. *Union Generals.* San Diego: Blackbirch Press, 2003.

Kelley, Brent P. *George McClellan: Union General.* Broomall, Pa.: Chelsea House Publishers, 2001.

Kent, Zachary. *William Seward: The Mastermind of the Alaska Purchase.* Berkeley Heights, N.J.: Enslow Publishers, Inc., 2001.

Kops, Deborah. *Abraham Lincoln.* Woodbridge, Conn.: Blackbirch Press, 2001.

Lutz, Norma Jean. *Frederick Douglass: Abolitionist and Author.* Philadelphia: Chelsea House Publishers, 2001.

Marrin, Albert. *Commander in Chief Abraham Lincoln and the Civil War.* New York: Dutton Children's Books, 1997.

McKissack, Fredrick L., and Patricia C. McKissack. *Days of Jubilee: The End of Slavery in the United States.* New York: Scholastic Press, 2003.

McPherson, James M. *Fields of Fury: the American Civil War.* New York: Atheneum Books for Young Readers, 2002.

Ojeda, Auriana. *The Civil War: 1850–1895.* vol. 5. Farmington Hills, Mich.: Gale Group, 2001.

Schuman, Michael A. *Ulysses S. Grant.* Berkeley Heights, N.J.: Enslow Publishers, Inc., 2004.

Whitelaw, Nancy. *William Tecumseh Sherman: Defender and Destroyer.* Greensboro, N.C.: Morgan Reynolds Inc., 2004.

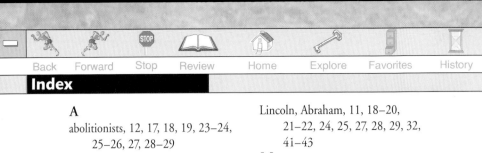
A

abolitionists, 12, 17, 18, 19, 23–24, 25–26, 27, 28–29

Antietam, Battle of, 21–22, 28, 43

Army of Northern Virginia, 32

Army of the Potomac, 32, 41, 43, 44

Army of the Tennessee, 35

B

Brown, John, 17–18

Bull Run, First Battle of, 35, 41

Bull Run, Second Battle of, 43, 45

C

Chase, Salmon P., 22–25

Chattanooga campaign, 11, 35, 39

Cold Harbor, Battle of, 32

Compromise of 1850, 15–16, 19, 25, 27

Cumberland, Department of the, 38

D

Davis, Jefferson, 42

Douglas, Stephen A., 19

Douglass, Frederick, 28–29

E

Emancipation Proclamation, 22, 26, 28

F

Fredericksburg, Battle of, 45

G

Gettysburg, Battle of, 32, 45

Grant, Ulysses S., 10–11, 22, 30–34, 35, 36, 37, 39, 45

H

Halleck, Henry W., 11

Hood, John Bell, 37, 39

Hooker, Joseph, 45

J

Johnston, Joseph E., 36–37, 42

K

Kansas-Nebraska Act, 16–17, 19, 24–25

L

Lee, Robert E., 21–22, 30, 32, 33, 38, 42, 43, 45

Lincoln, Abraham, 11, 18–20, 21–22, 24, 25, 27, 28, 29, 32, 41–43

M

McClellan, George, 11, 21–22, 30, 41–43

Meade, George G., 30, 32, 44–45

Mexican-American War, 10, 30, 34, 37, 41

Mill Springs, Battle of, 38

Missouri Compromise, 14–15

N

Nashville, Battle of, 39

P

Petersburg, siege of, 33

Pope, John, 43

R

Reconstruction, 34

S

Scott, Dred, 17

Scott, Winfield, 11, 30, 41

secession, 19

Seminole Wars, 37

Seven Days Battles, 44

Seven Pines, Battle of, 42

Seward, William H., 18, 26–28

Sherman, William Tecumseh, 30, 34–37, 39

Shiloh, Battle of, 11, 35

slavery, 12–13, 14–17

Sumner, Charles, 25–26

T

Thomas, George H., 30, 37–40

Trent Affair, 27–28

U

United States Military Academy at West Point, 10, 30, 34, 37, 41, 44

United States Supreme Court, 22

V

Vicksburg campaign, 11, 32, 35

W

War of 1812, 30

Wilderness, Battle of the, 32